# CONTENTS

I0200651

# QUICK QUOTES

## 700 INSPIRATIONAL QUOTES
## FOR PEOPLE ON THE GO

### HAMP LEE III

(com)mission™
PUBLISHING

Quick Quotes: 700 Inspirational Quotes for People on the Go
Hamp Lee III / 1st ed.

ISBN 978-1-940042-41-1

QUICK
QUOTES™
est. June 1998

# INTRODUCTION

Quick Quotes began in June 1998 as a daily e-mail ministry to friends and family. Since 1998, I've sent thousands of quotes around the world with a desire to inspire people to live for God and share His love with others.

I wrote *Quick Quotes: 700 Inspirational Quotes for People on the Go* as an inspirational resource along your journey as a Christian. As the title describes, each of us are on the *go*. We cross paths at different junctions of our lives, while heading to specific destinations, whether mentally, physically, emotionally, or spiritually. As our ultimate destination is the eternal city being prepared for us, I pray these seven hundred quotes will be a tremendous blessing in your life. May these quotes encourage, strengthen, challenge, and inspire you to live for God each day.

If you would like to receive Quick Quotes messages throughout the week, please follow me on Twitter, @spiritualcombat or register your e-mail at www.spiritualcombatants.com/quotes.

# ACCEPTANCE

Accept others for who they are, not what you want them to be.

You do not have to be smart, rich, pretty, or perfect to be loved and accepted by God.

# ADVERSITY

Adversity is one of the best teachers for building godly character.

# ADVICE

Do not place the word of man above the Word of God.

Surround yourself with good counsel and heed the advice you receive.

# ANGER

Acting out in anger will blind you from the path of righteousness.

Anger is a choice.

Anger is contagious.

Do not allow anger to be one of your advisors.

Do not allow anger to control your decisions.

Do not become a prisoner to the chains of anger.

Do not cause another person to have a bad day just because you are having one.

Unrestrained anger is a friend of sin.

When anger is your compass, you can be led in the wrong direction.

# ANSWERS

God will answer the questions on your heart in the right time and season of your life.

# APPRECIATION

Show your appreciation for others through gestures of love, service, and support.

# APPROVAL

Live to please your Heavenly Father.

Seek the approval of the Lord and not man.

Silence can often be perceived as an act of approval.

# ARGUMENTS

Turn from the desire to argue and gossip. Plant seeds of peace instead.

# ASSUMPTION

Assumptions can misguide your decisions.

Be careful when allowing assumptions to become your reality. Assumptions are not always based on truth.

Do not be quick to assume.

# ATTITUDE

A positive attitude is contagious, just as a negative attitude.

# BELIEVE

If only you will believe...

Nothing is impossible for God.

# BIBLE

A departure from the Word of God is a departure from your source of life, joy, and peace.

Allow the Bible to shape your life in godliness.

Allow the Word of God to cleanse your life.

Be quick to follow God's commands.

Depend on the Bible for answers to life's dilemmas.

Depressed? Read your Bible.
Angry? Read your Bible.
Happy? Read your Bible.
Stressed? Read your Bible.
In need of hope? Read your...

Do not use the Word of God to manipulate people.

Fall in love with God's Word.

Gain an understanding of the entire Bible.

Reading the Bible can comfort your soul in the best and worst of times.

The beauty of God's Word is found in the lives of its followers.

The path of true freedom is found in God's Word.

Understanding the Bible is a responsibility of all believers in Jesus Christ.

You cannot fall when you stand on the Word of God.

# BITTERNESS

Remove the root of bitterness and offense before they spread to your heart, mind, and soul.

# BLESSINGS

Be a blessing to someone today.

Do not withhold a blessing when it is in your ability to provide one.

See a need...meet the need.

This is the day the Lord has made...for you to be blessed and be a blessing to others.

You are deserving of God's blessings. Please accept His display and outpouring of love.

You do not need superpowers, gifts, or talents to be a blessing to others.

Your greatest blessing may come in the most unexpected package.

# CHANGE

A fear of change can chain you to your past.

A key ingredient of change is sacrifice.

Change begins with a *yes*.

Change comes with no guarantees, but when you think about it, it is probably better than where you are now.

Do not just think change. Be change!

Give people the opportunity to change instead of reminding them of their former self.

It is not too late to become a godly person.

Let change begin with you.

Make an inward decision for an outward change.

Mountains of change can be overcome using a spoon.

Overturn yesterday's mistakes.

Prayer is a key ingredient of change.

The change you want to see in others must first be witnessed in yourself.

The process of change begins in the mind.

You cannot force people to change.

You do not have to wait until the New Year to have a new resolution.

# CHARACTER

A good character is a priceless commodity.

A good name takes a lot longer to establish than to lose.

Allow your life to be defined by integrity, honesty, and compassion.

Never underestimate the value of having a good name.

# CHILDREN

Children do not need to mimic us, we need to mimic them (Matthew 18:1-4).

The joyful spirit of children warms the heart.

The life you display before children is often reflected in them.

# CHRISTIAN LIVING

A life in Christ is not centered around you.

Allow your standard of living to come from Jesus Christ.

Appreciate the little things in life.

Be more patient, loving, and forgiving than you were yesterday.

Be teachable.

Being a Christian is not like a light switch.

Do not allow negative people to pull you down to their level.

Do not allow small issues to become big distractions.

Do not dim your light in the midst of a dark world.

Do not live after the flesh. Live by the Spirit.

Doing what's right in public pleases people. Doing what's right in private pleases God.

God is not going to force you to live for Him. You have to want it for yourself.

Grow in grace and obedience to God and His Word.

Keep your eyes on the Lord.

Laughter is medicine. Love is life. Jesus is all.

Live at peace with those around you.

Live to please the Lord.

Live with boundaries.

Live your life in such a manner that it causes others to praise God.

Live your life in truth and integrity.

Many people struggle in their walk with the Lord because they are unwilling to commit to Him fully.

May your pursuit of God lead others deeper and closer to His heart.

Take heed to life's warning signs.

The power of God is seen in miraculous events through people like you.

The standard for how you treat others should not be based on how they treat you.

When riding on the road of faith, do not forget to enjoy the view.

You are Jesus' representative in your home, at work, and in your community.

Your actions will say more about your beliefs than your words.

Your life before God is your responsibility to live. Each of us will account for our own actions.

# CHURCH

A church in love with God will reveal Him to the world.

Allow people to be free to worship the Lord.

Allow your church to be a place of refuge.

Outreach is not a ministry but a lifestyle.

The family of God is not based on someone's color, race, socioeconomic status, or denomination.

There is a difference between being in church and being the church.

# COMFORT

Allow the Word of God to comfort you.

God has not forgotten you.

# COMMITMENT

A commitment to righteousness is not a one-time event.

Follow through on your promises and commitments.

Keep your focus on the prize which is found in Christ Jesus.

# COMMUNICATION

*Please* and *thank you* are pathways to peace.

Do not be afraid or ashamed to speak God's truth.

Good communication is a foundation of relationships.

Let your speech be worthy of being kept in the memory of others.

There are times when silence is the best answer.

Words come with no refunds or exchanges, so choose them carefully.

# COMMUNITY

Be aware of your surroundings.

Strive to improve your community.

# COMPASSION

Judgment divides. Compassion unifies.

When dealing with people, do not forget the grace the Lord has shown you.

# COMPLAINING

Complaining is a friend of separation, disharmony, and anger.

# CONFLICT

Be quick to settle disagreements and conflicts.

If you plant seeds of discord in your neighbor's yard, their roots will someday reach your yard.

# CONTENTMENT

Contentment is not based on the abundance of material things.

Find contentment in living righteously before the Lord.

# CONVICTION

Take heed to the conviction of the Holy Spirit.

# CORRECTION

Correct people out of love and not malice or hate.

If you are going to tell someone he or she is doing something wrong, take the time to tell him or her how to do it right.

Words of correction sting, but do not forget they are meant to heal you and make you whole.

# DEATH

Death is when true life begins.

# DECISIONS/GUIDANCE

A life of sin or righteousness is only a decision away.

Anger is a choice.
Hate is a choice.
Unforgiveness is a choice.
Love is a choice.
Laughter is a choice.
Choose wisely today.

Be led by the Lord and not society.

Be mindful of your sources of advice and counsel.

Before you make a decision, pray about it.

Do not allow interruptions in *your* schedule to sprout ungodly behavior.

Do not allow little issues to become big problems.

Do not allow public opinion to sway your decisions.

Do not allow your desires to override sound judgment.

Do not be hasty to make a decision. You may miss the mark of God's will.

Do not be quick to give an opinion.

Do not live your life as if you will always receive a second (third, fourth, fifth...) chance.

Do not take on more than you can handle.

Frustration can cloud sound judgment.

God will never give you bad advice.

Hatred and revenge are not proper influences for making decisions.

How would Jesus handle your situation?

If you agree to do something, why complain about it?!

If you choose to do something, give your best effort.

Make a conscious and continuous decision to serve the Lord.

One decision can change the course of your life.

Pay attention to the signs the Lord places on your path.

Remaining silent is sometimes shown as an act of approval.

Respond to difficult situations with the Word of God.

Taking a few extra moments to pray and think through a decision can save you a lot of time, energy, money, and peace.

Taking shortcuts in life does not guarantee success.

Free choice is a precious gift.

The person you will be tomorrow needs you to make wise decisions today.

The right decision may be hard to make, but it is still the right thing to do.

When a tough choice comes your way, have the courage to make the right decision.

Your tongue can be an instrument of peace or war.

# DELIVERANCE

Trust God for your deliverance.

# DESIRES

Do not give up on your desire to improve your life before God.

Your desire should never override the Lord's will.

# DISCIPLESHIP

Discipleship is not a one-time event.

How can people know you are Jesus' disciple if you are unwilling to love others?

# DISCIPLINE

Discipline can be used to correct or protect.

Do not despise the rod of correction.

If you are too hard on people, they will break.

Self-discipline is the denial of things detrimental to your well-being.

Set personal boundaries in order to protect you from you and others.

# DISTRACTION

Do not allow your life to distract people from the Lord and His will.

# DOUBT

Seeds of doubt will spoil a harvest.

# DREAMS

Do not allow your dreams to be shackled by your current surroundings.

# EDUCATION

Knowledge is a key that unlocks many doors in life.

Never stop learning.

Remain open to learning more about yourself.

# EMOTIONS

Do not allow your emotions to imprison you.

# ENCOURAGEMENT

A word of encouragement costs nothing to give.

Allow today to be a stepping stone to great things.

Develop a positive outlook on life...it's contagious.

Learn what motivates people, and then become their biggest encourager.

Make someone smile today.

Seek accountability that encourages you to remain on the path of righteousness.

Send a word of encouragement to someone you have not heard from in a while.

The Lord has not forgotten about you.

Use your position and influence to encourage others.

You are loved by God.

You can make a difference in the world.

# ENEMIES

How a person treats his or her enemies is an indication of his or her commitment to Jesus Christ.

Pray for your enemies.

The bridges you burn today, may need to be crossed tomorrow.

# ETERNITY

God's desire is to prepare you to live with Him forever.

Set your heart on the life to come and not the things of the world.

Set your sights on your heavenly home.

# EVANGELISM

Brag about God's mercy, grace, and love.

Do not allow internal or external influences to silence your testimony.

Do not allow the Great Commission to be an omission in your life.

God can be taken out of every public place, but He cannot be taken out of you.

There are people around you that need to know about Jesus.

# EXAMPLE

There are people around you that need to see your example of Christ-like living.

# EXCELLENCE

Be a person of excellence and integrity.

Excellence is not a one-time event.

Strive for excellence.

# FAITH

A decision made in faith is not determined by what is seen.

A little faith makes a big difference.

Be faithful to your responsibilities. People are depending on you.

Consider how faithful the Lord has been in your life.

Do not allow your feelings to dismantle your faith.

Faith moves toward God in spite of the hardships of life.

God is faithful in the best and worst of times.

Speak words of faith and not doubt.

# FAMILY/MARRIAGE

A community is built on the strength (and weakness) of its families.

A happy home is framed with love, patience, and the Word of God.

A home should be a sanctuary away from the turmoil of the outside world.

A marriage will not fix itself.

Create a home where love and peace can dwell.

Family time should never be considered a waste of time.

One of the most precious gifts you can give your family is your time.

Quality time with your family is always a good investment.

Spend memorable moments with your friends and family.

With God, no marriage is impossible from saving!

# FEAR

Do not allow the fear of man to steer your decisions.

The fear of the Lord will keep you off the path of sin.

# FELLOWSHIP

Be mindful of the company you keep.

Fellowship with people that aspire to live for God.

Make time for fellowship.

# FLESH

The flesh is not interested in living righteously before God.

The flesh has no fear of God.

# FOCUS

With so many distractions in the world, keep your focus on the Lord.

# FORGIVENESS

Do not allow the pain of disappointment, betrayal, or offense to keep you from loving others.

Do not allow unforgiveness to affect your relationship with God.

Everyone deserves God's love and forgiveness.

Forgiveness is a decision founded in love.

Forgiveness is medicine for the soul.

Forgiveness is treating a person as if he or she never wronged you.

There is beauty in forgiveness. It reflects the character of God.

There is forgiveness in Jesus.

There is freedom in forgiveness.

You are worthy of forgiveness.

You cannot forgive without love.

# FRIENDSHIP

Be the friend you want others to be to you.

Friends help you see where you are not looking, assist you when you fall, lend their shoulder to cry on, and give you an honest answer.

True friends will not ask you to live outside of God's will.

# GIFTS/TALENTS

Do not allow the gifts and talents God gives you to go unused.

People cannot disqualify a God-given gift or talent.

Talents and gifts are meant to be shared.

Three great gifts you can give another person is your time, a listening ear, and your support.

# GIVING

A heart to give begins with love to share.

Appreciate the little things people give to you.

Give thanks by giving to others.

Give without expecting anything in return.

Giving inspires hope in the giver and the recipient.

Giving is an outward display of inward love.

Your giving may be the answer someone prayed for.

# GLORIFYING GOD

Give glory to God in the midst of trials and tribulations.

Unexpected interruptions are opportunities for God to be glorified.

# GOALS

Determination is the engine that propels you toward your goals.

Do not sabotage another person's dream or goal.

# GOD

Do not limit God.

God is amazing.

God is preparing you for His glory.

God never fails.

Never underestimate what God can do.

No situation is too big or small for the Lord.

We need God in our lives.

What is seen does not limit God.

# GOD'S CREATION

You are special. You were created by God.

# GOD'S WILL

God can make a way where none currently exists.

God's will for your life may be different than you imagined.

In a world that screams for attention, seek the quiet voice of the Lord.

In fulfilling God's will, you must free yourself of personal agendas and desires.

The Lord is faithful to perform His Word.

The slightest distraction can steer you from God's will.

You are never in the wrong place when you are in the center of God's will.

# GODLINESS

A lifestyle of godliness begins at home.

Godliness is intentional.

# GOSSIP

Do not be a conduit for gossip.

Gossip causes you to forget that people are in need of prayer and God's mercy and grace.

Gossip strips people of their dignity.

Instead of gossiping about people, pray for them.

# GRACE

God's grace can sustain you.

Through mistakes and mercy, we learn about the expansive love of God.

# GROWTH

In every opportunity or challenge you face, there is something to be learned.

It is important to provide people with enough *space* to grow.

The seeds you plant in someone's life today, can grow to feed others tomorrow.

# HAPPINESS

Laughter is a doorway to peace.

Laughter is healing for the soul.

# HATE

Hate erodes your ability to see the beauty in life.

Hate may seem like an unbreakable wall, but love conquers all.

Hatred binds the hands of peace.

Hatred scars the fabric of your heart and soul.

Life is too short to hate people.

To hate someone is to pour cement on your heart.

# HEALING

God still heals.

Thankfulness and forgiveness brightens the soul and heals the heart.

# HEART

A hardened heart shackles your life without the possibility of freedom.

A heart of grace is seasoned with compassion.

Do not harden your heart toward the conviction of the Holy Spirit.

Have a grateful heart.

# HELP

Allow the Lord to be your source of help and support.

As the Lord delivers you out of difficult times and seasons, do not forget to reach back to help others.

Be a person that improves the lives of everyone around you.

Be sensitive to the circumstances and situations of others.

Do not be too afraid, ashamed, or prideful to ask for help.

Do not look down on the less fortunate. Help them to stand.

God can open and close any door in your life.

Help others to realize their potential.

Keep your eyes on the Lord and not your problems.

Never underestimate the help you can give. Even the smallest deed can have a big impact.

No matter how truthful, some opinions are not well received by its recipient.

Take the time to help someone that is struggling.

Take time to teach and empower others.

You cannot make people accept your help.

# HOLINESS

Holiness is a continual commitment throughout each day, in every situation.

Holiness is a standard within everyone's reach.

Live a consecrated life before the Lord and His people.

The Lord has not lowered His standard.

# HOPE

Do not lose hope for a better tomorrow.

Hope lifts you above the ashes of despair.

Let your hope rest securely in Jesus.

No one is hopeless who hopes in God.

# HUMILITY

Humility is one of the greatest assets for a disciple of Jesus.

# INSPIRATION

Inspire people through your actions.

# INTEGRITY

Do what is right...even if no one else does.

# INTIMACY

Intimacy with the Lord begins with the denial of self.

When you do not have intimacy with God, you lack compassion for people.

# JESUS

Celebrate Jesus today and forever.

Jesus Christ is the most important person in the history of the world.

Jesus died so that you may be free from the wages of sin and death.

Jesus is all you need.

# JOY

If your joy is stolen, it does not leave without your consent.

The joy of children warms the heart.

# JUDGING

When you judge someone, your ability to love him or her is diminished.

# LAZINESS

Fight the appetites of procrastination and laziness.

Many people are willing to reap the benefits of hard work, yet are not willing to work hard.

# LEADERSHIP

Leadership begins with prayer.

Serve and support those placed in your care.

Take a moment to thank those who serve behind the scenes.

Use the authority and influence you have been given (at whatever level) to improve the lives of those around you.

# LIFE

A life lived for Christ is a life well-spent.

An inspection of your life is worthless if you do nothing about your findings.

Do not allow Satan to be pleased with your life.

Do not be slow to read the Bible, slow to pray, and quick to become angry because things do not go your way.

Every life is precious in the eyes of God.

Fill your day with peace, joy, and laughter.

If your life seems like its sinking, you must throw some things overboard.

Life is too short for drama.

Live this day to please the Lord.

Live your life in integrity and truth.

May your private life reveal the love and glory of God.

Minimize distractions.

Set your life on pleasing God.

There are many shortcuts in life that will take you nowhere.

Today can be your best day yet.

Today is not just another day.

Why put off what can be done today when tomorrow is not promised to you?

Your actions are not hidden from God.

Your life in Christ should say you believe long before your words do.

# LISTEN

Be an attentive listener.

Give people an opportunity to tell their story.

Sometimes your family and friends need you to listen and not speak.

# LOVE

Acts of love are contagious.

Allow love to be the main ingredient in your life.

As you desire to be loved, understood, and appreciated, remember that your neighbor does as well.

Create an atmosphere where God's love can dwell and flow freely.

Do not allow the world's standard of love to become your own.

Everyone has a desire to be loved.

God can use anyone to reveal His love, mercy, and grace.

God is love.

God's love is for everyone.

God's love is meant for the world to receive and enjoy.

God's love is meant for you.

Love cannot be purchased with money.

Love carries an eraser.

Love considers the needs of others first.

Love costs nothing to give but its return on investment is priceless.

Love does not exclude people.

Love does not force someone to do something he or she does not want to do.

Love does not give up on others.

Love gives the best it has to offer.

Love has no boundaries.

Love is a sacrifice of self.

Love is not a bystander.

Love is not a one-time event.

Love is not concerned about the color of your skin, the money in your pockets, or your social status.

Love people enough to tell them about Jesus.

Love prays for others.

Love shows us a better way.

Love speaks louder than words.

Love will never be overrated.

Loving your enemy is a choice.

Prejudice, gossip, and love are contagious. Which one will you spread?

Show the world you love God by your actions.

The beauty of God's love can be found with one look in the mirror.

The depth of God's love is limitless.

The natural response of love is giving.

The strength for loving difficult people is founded in your love for God.

True love is not selfish.

Unconditional love accepts people *as is*.

# LYING

Lying breaks down boundaries of trust.

Lying is not an escape from the truth.

# MATURITY

A life of maturity is developed as one submits to the Holy Spirit.

Accepting responsibility for your actions is a sign of personal growth.

The Lord uses trying situations to help you mature and trust in Him more.

# MERCY

Thank God for His mercy.

# MINISTRY

Be available.

Do not despise small and humble beginnings. God is preparing you for His glory.

Fill your life with people that will pour into you and those you can pour into.

God can use anyone to reveal His love, mercy, and grace.

Show the same level of care, respect, and support for the *least* and the *greatest* of people.

There is no *me* in ministry.

# MONEY

Be wise in your spending.

Having the wrong relationship with money will disrupt your relationship with God and His will for your life.

Live within your means.

Make a habit of saving a little from each paycheck rather than finding creative ways to spend every dime you have.

Money can only buy stuff, not true happiness.

Money cannot buy godly character.

Money does not define who you are.

# MOTIVES

Allow your motives to be pure before the Lord and man.

The reason why you do something is just as important as the act itself.

# MUSIC

Be mindful of the music you listen to. Music can free or imprison your soul.

Fill your soul with music that will draw you closer to the Lord and not the world.

For worship leaders: sing to praise and worship the Lord and lead others to do the same instead of attempting to bring praise and worship to yourself.

# NEW BEGINNINGS

Allow your success to begin with God.

Every day is a new beginning.

This is the day to show *yesterday* that your past is truly behind you.

Today is a good day for a fresh start.

# OBEDIENCE

A time may come when God asks you to do something that makes absolutely no sense to you or anyone else, but you still must obey His voice.

Allow your satisfaction to come from pleasing God.

Do not delay a decision to be obedient to the Lord.

Give the Lord your full attention.

Live in greater submission to the Lord.

Many things God will ask of you will not come with an explanation. Be obedient and walk faithfully before Him.

Your obedience to God will be an outpouring of blessings to others.

# OFFENSE

Being offended is like a prison—no one gets in and you do not get out.

Do not allow differences of opinion to create walls of separation and offense.

# OPPORTUNITIES

Make the most of your opportunities, for some do not come around a second time.

Opportunities to be a blessing to others exist all around you.

# OVERCOMING

Confront the childhood issues that disrupt your adult life.

Do not allow negative situations to define you. Rise above them.

The life of a believer is one of overcoming.

You can overcome the pain of your past.

# PATIENCE

A key ingredient of dealing with people is patience.

A little patience today can save you from a lot of trouble tomorrow.

A patient life is establish through trials.

A person that is patient is not judgmental.

Allow patience to change your perception.

An ounce of patience will reveal a pound of truth.

Be patient with people as the Lord has been patient with you.

Do not be discouraged by a delayed answer.

Do not settle for something just to say you have it. Be patient and wait for the Lord to provide.

Give God the opportunity to mold you and others into the image of His Son.

Have the courage to wait on the Lord.

Patience can outlast a man of strength.

Patience develops inner peace.

Patience opens doors tomorrow that are not seen today.

Patience reveals other perspectives beside your own.

When you have more questions than answers, be still. When things do not move fast enough, be still. Trust. Wait. Pray.

# PEACE

Silence can be used as an instrument of peace.

To find peace you have to lose hate, sin, and offense.

# PEOPLE

Appreciate the people in your life.

Be fair and honest when dealing with people.

Do not allow people to keep you from serving God.

Do not be quick to discard people.

Do not give up on people because they do not act the way you want. Do not forget the people that did not give up on you.

Do not look down on others.

Every person has value.

God made each person unique and special.

Hurting people hurt others.

Living to please people can keep you from pleasing the Father.

Spend time investing in others.

When dealing with others, ask yourself if you would like to be treated in a similar manner.

You were created for a purpose.

You are not the only one with problems. Be sensitive to others.

# PERSEVERANCE

Do not allow a painful past to keep you from living a fruitful future.

Do not allow the failures of others to be an excuse to give up.

Do not allow your past to affect who you are today and who God is calling you to become tomorrow.

Do not give up because the path ahead seems rough.

Do not give up on God.

Do not give up. Keep taking small steps in the right direction.

If you fall, be quick to dust yourself off and rise again.

Improve upon yesterday's shortcomings.

It takes faith and hope to believe your situation will not last always.

Perseverance is doing what needs to be done, even when you do not feel like doing it.

Stand above the shadows of disappointment and despair.

There are some things in life that can only be achieved through dedication, discipline, and perseverance. Shortcuts will not get you there.

You have come too far to quit now.

# PRAISE

Allow songs of praise to fill your heart.

Allow songs of praise to heal your soul.

Be thankful for the smallest gifts.

Do not allow your problems to keep you from praising God.

Let your praise to God be continuous.

Praise God for who He is and what He has done in your life.

Praise has the ability to place you beyond the *sting* of your circumstances.

Thank God for what you have. Trust God for what you need.

The Lord is worthy of praise in the best and worst of times.

There is much to be thankful for.

True praise is developed out of a trust and love for God.

# PRAYER

Allow prayer to be your first impulse and not a last resort.

Begin each day with prayer.

Cast every care and thought upon Jesus.

Do not allow prayer to be an afterthought.

Each person you know is in need of prayer. You never know what someone is going through.

God hears your prayers.

God knows the desires of your heart, and when He comes with an answer, do not be upset if it is not what you expected.

It costs nothing to pray for another person.

Never underestimate the power of (persevering) prayer.

Patient persistent prayer produces perfected people.

Pray as if you believe God heard your prayer and will answer it.

Pray before you act.

Pray for peace. Pray for love. Pray for forgiveness.

Pray for the people that hate you, try to sabotage your work, and always put you down. They need Jesus too.

Pray for your leaders.

Pray more. Talk less.

Prayer does change things. Often it begins with you and how you see your situations.

Prayer is never overrated.

Share the pains of your heart with the Lord. He can heal the deepest hurt and help you discover freedom and wholeness.

Some people will not receive your words, but God will accept your prayers.

Sometimes you need to quiet your soul in the Father's presence.

Sometimes...the only thing you can do is pray.

Take time in prayer to listen to the Lord.

When a person comes to your mind (especially someone you have not seen in a while), say a prayer for them.

When you do not know what to do...pray. When you know what to do...pray.

You can speak to God about anything. Try it now.

# PREJUDICE

There is no discrimination or prejudice in Jesus.

# PREPARATION

God will use *anyone* and *anything* to teach you. Do not despise the manner and method of His preparation.

Trust the path and process of your season. God is preparing you for His glory.

# PRIDE

Never be too big to ask for help or receive instruction from others.

Pride blinds you from the obstacles in your own path.

Pride keeps you from saying, I love you, I'm sorry, I was wrong, please forgive me, can we start again...

# PRIORITIES

Allow God's desire for your life to be your top priority.

Allow the Lord to set your priorities.

Inventory the priorities you have in your life.

There are many distractions in life. Stick to your priorities.

Your greatest priority in life should be your relationship with your Father in Heaven.

# PROBLEMS

Having a problem is sometimes a matter of your perspective.

Treat the source of your problems, not just the symptoms.

# PROMISE

Hold onto the promises the Lord has given you...regardless of how circumstances might seem. Do not faint or give up.

The Lord keeps His promise.

# PROVISION

God provides.

God will provide everything you need to fulfill your purpose in Him.

# PURPOSE

In order to discover your true purpose in life, you must place your full trust in God.

No one was born by accident.

You were created with purpose for a purpose.

# REFLECTION

Be willing to see another point of view besides your own.

Spend a few moments reflecting on God's involvement in your life.

Use quiet moments in the day to refresh, reflect, and refocus.

# RELATIONSHIPS

A friend of questionable character can lead you astray.

Address people as if it will be the last time you will see them.

Allow Jesus Christ to be the foundation of your relationships.

Be quick to apologize and mend relationships.

Be quick to heal wounded relationships.

Be selective of the people you allow to *speak* into your life (i.e. friends, TV/radio personalities, etc.).

Be someone people can count on.

Be thankful for the people you can call your friends...including Jesus.

Build relationships based on love not rules and regulations.

Do not allow miscommunication to strain a relationship.

Do not be afraid to represent Jesus among your peers.

Do not be quick to enter friendships or partnerships.

Do not treat people unfairly because they do not do what you want them to do.

Establish (and maintain) proper relationship boundaries.

Find ways to enrich the relationships in your life.

People are not worthless.

Someone is depending on you to be honest, faithful, loving, fair, patient, and forgiving.

Surround yourself with friends that lift you, encourage you, support you, and tell you the truth.

Take the first step to restore a relationship.

Take time to appreciate the people around you.

The way people treat you should not determine how you will treat them.

Treat people with respect—regardless of their race, position, or status.

When you learn something new, share it with someone.

# REPENTANCE

Be quick to repent and turn from sin.

# RESPONSIBILITY

Do not run from responsibility...embrace it.

Manage your resources and the positions you hold with honesty and integrity.

Uphold your responsibilities.

# REST

Be attentive to your spiritual, physical, emotional, and mental temperament.

Find healthy (and sin-free) outlets to relieve stress.

Know when you need to give yourself a timeout.

Restoration can be found in the presence of the Lord.

Take a day each week to rest from the weariness of life.

# REVENGE

Do not treat people badly for something someone else did to you.

Overcome the desire to act out of revenge and hate.

Respond to evil with good.

The best *revenge* is to love instead of hate, support instead of sabotage, and forgive instead of offend.

Vindication comes from the Lord.

# RIGHTEOUSNESS

Saturate your life with righteousness.

# SACRIFICE

In order to win in this life, your flesh will have to lose.

Victory does not come without sacrifice and dedication.

# SALVATION

Even before you knew the Lord, He knew you and was working to draw you closer to Himself.

Give people an opportunity to work out their salvation.

Jesus died so that you may be free from the wages of sin and death.

Jesus paid the price for your salvation.

# SEEKING GOD

God is available to everyone that seeks Him.

# SELF-AWARENESS

Know your strengths and weaknesses.

Remain open to learning more about yourself.

# SELF-CONTROL

A lack of self-control can bring a loss of credibility and trust.

A lack of self-control is a sign of weakness.

A life without self-control will become out of control.

Self-discipline is the denial of things detrimental to your well-being and soul.

The only person you can truly control is yourself.

With self-discipline come great rewards.

# SELF-WORTH

You are not worthless.

Your worth is not determined by the money in your bank account, clothes in your closet, your job title, or things you can buy.

# SELFISHNESS

Selfish behavior is incompatible with serving God.

Selfishness is an enemy of godliness.

The aftertaste of selfishness is sin.

# SERVICE

A life completely dedicated to Christ is one well served.

Allow the Lord to use you to be His hands, feet, heart, and mouthpiece to the world.

Be diligent in your work, compassionate in your service, and loving in your home.

Do not forget to care for the volunteers that serve within your midst.

Do not underestimate the impact you can make in your home, workplace, and community.

Give the best of your day to serving others.

Serving God should not be an afterthought.

Serving God is not a sign of weakness.

Your service to others is developed from your love and commitment to the Lord.

# SIN

A guarantee of sin is death.

A taste of sin can lead to a lifetime of regret.

Do not tempt anyone to sin.

Drawing closer to Jesus means moving away from the world and sin.

Sin blinds you from the possibility of hope.

Sin will never be worth its wages.

Walk away from situations that might lead to sin.

You do not have to sin.

# SORROW

Do not rejoice over someone else's misery.

# SPEAKING

Choose your words carefully.

Let the words you speak manifest from the Word of God.

Let your words and actions be seasoned with love.

Let your words be few, yet meaningful.

Watch what you say because people are listening and can be influenced by your words.

# STARTING OVER

A fresh start begins with a fresh thought.

Allow today to be a stepping stone to great things.

Do not allow what other people say about you to define who you can become.

Do not be afraid to start over.

Lord...renew me today.

When starting over, start small, but remain consistent.

# STRENGTH

Allow the Lord to strengthen you.

Draw your strength from the Lord.

# SUCCESS

Celebrate the success of others.

Help others find their success.

If you want to be great, be a great father or mother, husband or wife, brother or sister, co-worker or friend, and child of God.

There are no overnight successes. Success begins in the halls of small beginnings. Be faithful in the small things.

# SUFFERING

Temporary pleasure (in the flesh), eternal loss. Temporary pain (in the flesh) for God's glory, eternal gain.

# SUPPORT

Allow your service and support to be given without cost.

Be a source of encouragement, help, and support for those in need.

Consider the interests of others above your own.

Supporting another person may amount to nothing more than your presence.

# TEMPTATION

Answer temptation with the Word of God.

Be watchful for temptation. It reveals itself in different ways.

Do not give temptation the attention it desires.

It only takes the brain a split second to produce thoughts and feelings of something you glanced at...guard yourself.

Running away from temptation is a sign of strength, not weakness.

Stay on your guard against temptation.

When temptation comes, look to the Lord instead of focusing on the temptation.

# TESTIMONY

One of the ways you can share your faith with others is by telling your life story and testimony.

# THANKFULNESS

Celebrate the small victories in life.

Enjoy everything God has given you.

Give thanks for all the Lord has done.

Take a moment to give thanks to God.

# THINKING

A mind without peace cannot focus.

Allow positive thoughts to fill your life with hope and expectancy.

Be quick to think positive. Have faith. Believe.

In order to be different, you must first think different.

Keep your mind active on Christ.

Reduce negative thoughts and situations.

Take a stand against negative thoughts.

Untamed thoughts are dangerous to your soul.

Your perception of Jesus will affect your response to Him.

# TIME

Appreciate the time you have. There are no refunds.

Be respectful of other people's time.

Make the best use of your time and it will make the best of you.

One of the most precious gifts you can give is your time.

Sadly, time is most appreciated when there is little remaining.

Spend time quietly before the Lord.

You only have so much time and energy. Stop spending it on anger, hate, and revenge.

# TRUST

Trust God for everything.

Trusting God will require a release of your will.

Where there is trust in God, there is hope.

# TRUTH

Do not be afraid to tell the truth. It will offend some, but it has the ability to free many others.

Focus on truth. Read truth. Share truth. Follow truth.

Only lies and half-truths require an explanation. The truth stands on its own.

The truth does not hide its intentions.

The truth might sting, but it also heals.

You discern what is false by learning what is true.

# UNITY

Unity within the body of Christ is achievable.

# VISION

Breathe new life into your dreams and desires.

Do not lose sight of the vision God has given you.

# WISDOM

Wisdom can keep you free of many pitfalls and troubling situations.

# WORK

Allow your quality of work to reveal the contents of your character.

Give the Lord (and His people) the very best of what you have every day.

Let your hands be filled with abundant work.

Potential is worthless if not acted upon.

# WORLDLINESS

Do not allow the desire for money, positions, and possessions to consume you.

Do not allow the world to affect how you see God.

# WORRY

Worry blinds you from seeking a solution to your problems.

Worry detracts your mind from the ways of the Lord.

Worry restrains your ability to enjoy love, joy, and peace.

Worrying is a sign that your trust in God is not complete.

# WORSHIP

Worship the Lord through your obedience.

(com)mission

P U B L I S H I N G

www.commissionpubs.com

info@commissionpubs.com